Pirate Ships & Weapons

by John Hamilton

Visit us at
www.abdopublishing.com

Published by ABDO Publishing Company, 4940 Viking Drive, Suite 622, Edina, Minnesota 55435.
Copyright ©2007 by Abdo Consulting Group, Inc. International copyrights reserved in all countries.
No part of this book may be reproduced in any form without written permission from the publisher.
ABDO & Daughters™ is a trademark and logo of ABDO Publishing Company.

Printed in the United States.

Editor: Sue Hamilton
Graphic Design: John Hamilton
Cover Design: Neil Klinepier
Cover Illustration: *Blackbeard*, ©1996 Don Maitz; *Pegleg*, ©1996 Don Maitz
Interior Photos and Illustrations: p 1 *Ahoy Maitz*, ©2002 Don Maitz; schooner, Mariners' Museum;
p 3 *Dead Men Tell No Tales*, ©2003 Don Maitz; p 4 *On the Run*, ©2002 Don Maitz; p 5 *Crossed*
©2002 Don Maitz; p 6 (top) hanger, Corbis; (bottom) *Hooked Pirate*, ©2002 Don Maitz; p 7 (left)
Pegleg, ©1996 Don Maitz; (right) cutlass, Corbis; p 8 (top) marlinspike, Corbis; (bottom) axe, Corbis;
p 9 (top) dagger, Mariners' Museum; (bottom) pirate with knife, courtesy Pirate's Dinner Adventure;
p 10 flintlock pistol, Mariners' Museum; p 11 *Beach Party*, ©2004 Don Maitz; p 12 (top) flintlock
musket being fired, ©2001 John Hamilton; (bottom) blunderbuss, AP/Wideworld; p 13 *Far From
Home*, ©1997 Don Maitz; p 14 pirate skirmish, Mariners' Museum; p 15 *Then the Real Fight Began*,
Howard Pyle; p 17 pirate ship, Mariners' Museum; p 18 *Whydah*, ©1999 Don Maitz; pp 20-21
illustrations of ship types, courtesy *Pirates of the Burning Sea*/Flying Lab Software; p 24 man-of-war
with cannons, Corbis; p 25 *Gunner With Ball*, ©1996 Don Maitz; p 26 pirate mortally wounded,
Mariners' Museum; p 27 sailors exchange cannon fire with pirates, Mariners' Museum; pp 28-29 *Forty
Thieves*, ©1991 Don Maitz; p 31 *Patches*, ©2003 Don Maitz.

Library of Congress Cataloging-in-Publication Data

Hamilton, John, 1959-
    Pirate ships & weapons / John Hamilton.
        p. cm. -- (Pirates)
    Includes index.
    ISBN-13: 978-1-59928-763-8
    ISBN-10: 1-59928-763-3
    1. Pirates--Juvenile literature. 2. Sailing ships--Juvenile literature. 3. Weapons--Juvenile literature.
I. Title. II. Title: Pirate ships and weapons.

G535.H254 2007
910.4'5--dc22

                                        2006032015

Contents

Armed and Dangerous

A pirate's job was to steal and plunder. Most pirates, although they were ferocious and daring, were also very smart. They knew that the best way to take over a ship was by fear and intimidation. If they actually got into a fight, people became injured or were killed—including the pirates. It was much better to scare their victims into giving up without resisting, without shots being fired or swords being drawn.

When pirates maneuvered alongside rich merchant vessels, they ran the frightening Jolly Roger up the mast. They jeered and shouted curses. But they had to back up their bluster with sharp blades and powerful firearms. Pirates had weapons galore, mainly to intimidate their foes into surrendering. But they also knew that when their bluff was called, and a tense situation erupted into blood and thunder, it was better to be armed to the teeth. Instead of blasting another ship and ruining whatever plunder it might be carrying, it was better for pirates to board their quarry and fight the other crew in hand-to-hand combat. And heaven help a merchant crew that chose to fight pirates rather than surrender. Pirates were notorious for showing no mercy to victims who resisted.

Crossed (facing page) and *On the Run* (below), by famed pirate artist Don Maitz.

Blades

Fighting men of the sea have been using bladed weapons for thousands of years. Some of these weapons were originally used as tools for sailing, and were later adapted for combat. Other blades were first used in battle by soldiers on land, and were then eventually modified for the unique requirements of shipboard fighting.

Above: An example of a hanger, a type of short sword. *Below: Hooked Pirate* by Don Maitz.

Cutlasses

The familiar single-edged cutlass has been called the "sword of the seas." Compared to swords used by land-based soldiers, the cutlass had a shorter blade. It was also slightly heavier, and more sturdy. Not only did pirates use their cutlasses to "run through" their enemies, they also cut heavy ship ropes, or used the weapon's hilt to help break down cabin doors. A regular sword might easily break from this kind of abuse.

A cutlass has a slightly curving blade, which means it was used mainly to hack and slash at a pirate's foe. Straight-bladed swords and rapiers were used to stab, but the cutlass was a more straightforward weapon for men with limited sword-fighting experience. Instead of precisely stabbing at the heart or gut, a pirate could just as easily win by chopping off his opponent's hand. The cutlass' sturdy blade made cutting through bone and muscle much easier.

The short blade of the cutlass also made it ideal for fighting aboard ships, which became very crowded during battle. A longer sword did little good if was constantly getting tangled in a ship's rigging.

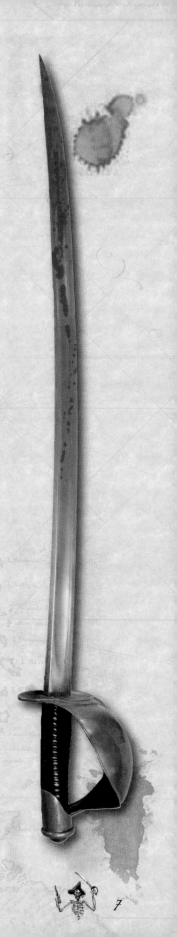

Above: *Pegleg* by Don Maitz.

Right: A navy cutlass had a sturdy, slightly curved blade that made it an ideal weapon for hand-to-hand combat aboard sailing vessels. Many pirate cutlasses had blades that were shorter and wider, which made them even more sturdy.

Above: A handy tool aboard a ship was a marlinspike, which could also be used as an effective weapon.

Marlinspikes

When fighting began aboard a ship, a sailor might find himself without his trusty cutlass. He would probably pick up whatever weapon he could find, and in many cases it was some kind of sailing tool. A marlinspike was similar in shape to an ice pick. Its thin, tapered end was jammed between strands of tightened rope in order to separate them. They were also used to anchor and secure lines attached to sails. A marlinspike made a very effective club when used in desperate hand-to-hand fighting. Some pirate captains feared mutinies from their own pirate crews, so they locked up the men's guns and knives in storage below deck. In such cases, mutineers often used marlinspikes as weapons. Since these items were necessary tools to run a ship, they were always close at hand.

Axes

Another common shipboard item was the axe. Normally used to cut lines and perform other chopping chores, a long-handled axe could be handy during ship-to-ship skirmishes.

Above: Axes could be used to cut the grappling lines of unwelcome pirates.

Defenders used axes to repel boarding parties by cutting through grappling lines, which were used to pull ships together. Attackers, once aboard their prey, used axes to chop down heavy doors and hatches, or cut rigging lines used to hold sails. Although slower than a cutlass, an axe also made a formidable weapon. But despite how they're often shown in Hollywood movies, boarding axes were not meant to be thrown. Smaller throwing hatchets and tomahawks eventually became common on ships, but not until about the end of the 18th century. In addition to being thrown, tomahawks were also easier to swing on crowded ships.

Knives and Daggers

Every pirate worth his salt carried one or more knives, either for shipboard chores or as a weapon during hand-to-hand combat.

A very large knife was called a gully, some of which folded like big pocket knives. Gullies were general-purpose knives, but could be used as weapons if needed.

Daggers were specifically designed for combat. Daggers had sharp points that were thrust at opponents. They were also used to parry, or block, an opponent's sword thrusts.

Many buccaneers of the Caribbean used *boucan* knives, which were originally used as hunting knives.

Above: A real pirate dagger.
Below: Some pirates fought with hunting knives, which were used to slash and hack at opponents.

Firearms

The flintlock pistol was the most common type of firearm used during the Golden Age of Piracy, from about 1660 to 1740. There were many types of flintlocks available. Pirates liked the short-barreled pistols, which could easily be stuffed in a belt or hidden in a coat.

To prepare a flintlock, the pirate had to first pour a measured amount of gunpowder down the barrel, followed by a wadding material and a round, lead ball. The ball and wadding created a tight seal inside the barrel. Flintlocks were clumsy and difficult to aim. To fire the pistol, more gunpowder was poured onto a priming pan. Then a spring-loaded doghead, which held a small piece of stone, called flint, was cocked back into position. When the trigger was pulled, the doghead

Right: A Belgian flintlock pistol. The short barrel would have made it easy for a pirate to conceal it in his belt or coat.

was released and snapped downward. It struck a piece of metal, called a frizzen, which created a spark and ignited the gunpowder. If the pirate's aim was true, the lead ball shot out of the flintlock's barrel and struck the target. Flintlocks made a loud "hiss-bang" noise when fired, and created a cloud of blue-white smoke that smelled like sulphur. Shipboard battles quickly became smoke-filled scenes of carnage.

Because it took so long to load flintlocks, many pirates kept two or more pistols fully loaded right before battle. The famous pirate Blackbeard was said to carry at least three flintlocks, each tied to his coat with silk sashes. When he fired a shot, he simply dropped the pistol and left it dangling. When he was out of pistols, he switched to his trusty cutlass and knife.

Above: Beach Party by artist Don Maitz.

Muskets

Like pistols, muskets were prized possessions of most pirates. The buccaneers of Hispaniola were crack shots, having trained for years using their muskets to hunt wild game. This skill translated very well to piracy. The Spanish, whose galleons were so often raided by buccaneers, thought that pirates were the best shots in the world.

Just like flintlock pistols, muskets had to be reloaded with gunpowder, ball, and wadding for every shot. During a frenzied ship-to-ship battle, it seemed to take forever to reload a musket. Still, these weapons did have distinct advantages. Muskets had a longer range and were more accurate than pistols. They could be fired accurately from a long distance while a pirate ship was maneuvering close to another vessel. The pirates hoped to clear the deck of their quarry to make it easier for the first wave of boarders to capture the targeted ship. At the same time, muskets could be used from a distance by merchant-ship sailors to repel boarding pirates.

Above: A flintlock musket being fired, at the moment the doghead hits the frizzen, igniting the gunpowder.

Blunderbusses

A blunderbuss was the ancestor to today's shotgun. Its name is Dutch for *donderbus*, which means "thunder gun." It was much shorter than a musket, with a characteristic funnel shape at the end of the muzzle.

Blunderbusses were flintlock weapons that shot small lead pellets, which scattered over a wide area at close range. Within about 30 feet (9.1 m), a blunderbuss was a devastating weapon. It fired with a loud roar, and anything within its kill zone was torn to shreds. Pirates found it very effective to fire a blunderbuss at the deck of their victims' ship before swinging over and fighting hand to hand.

Facing page: Far From Home by Don Maitz. *Below:* A blunderbuss.

Tooth and Nail

When pirates boarded other ships and began hand-to-hand combat, things got ugly fast. Unlike the fights depicted in Hollywood movies, real-life pirate battles were brutal, bloody, and filled with cruelty and pain.

The majority of pirates were regular sailors before joining ranks with their piratical brethren. They were not very well trained in the art of swordplay. When a pirate and his victim fought, they hacked away at each other with whatever weapon they could find, either a sword, an axe, a knife, or even a sailing tool such as a belaying pin, normally used to secure ropes but excellent in combat when used as a club.

Many buccaneers were skilled marksmen, having spent years hunting wild game on forested islands such as Hispaniola. But after the first shots were fired, there was little time to reload, and men resorted to the glint of sharp steel.

In the middle of a melee, a ship became a terrible place. Thick smoke and the sulphur smell of gunpowder hung in the air. The wooden deck became slippery with blood, and the shouts and screams of injured men rang out.

Right: Pirates swarm aboard a vessel and fight in hand-to-hand combat.

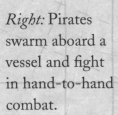

Above: Then the Real Fight Began by Howard Pyle. Note the belaying pin used by the wounded pirate.

Pirate Ships

Pirate ships were not made to order—they were stolen. During the Golden Age of Piracy, in the Caribbean Sea especially, pirates routinely seized regular cargo ships. Prize ships were sometimes sold. Others were sunk, or set adrift. Oftentimes, however, the captured vessels were modified to serve as new pirate ships.

Pirates looked for certain traits in choosing a ship. It had to be fast in order to catch prey, or to run from the authorities. Smaller and lighter ships were generally faster and more maneuverable. For this reason, many pirates preferred sloops, which were small, fast ships, with a single mast capable of spreading a huge amount of sail. The sloops built by shipwrights in Bermuda and Jamaica were especially prized. Their red cedar hulls were very strong, and could easily support the weight of extra cannons if the pirates wished to modify the ships' armaments.

Pirate ships also had to be seaworthy, capable of traveling long voyages in rough weather. The pirate Bartholomew Roberts, for example, traveled great distances across the Atlantic Ocean, from Africa to the Caribbean to the northern island of Newfoundland, in search of plunder.

Pirates also valued a ship with a shallow draft, which meant it could sail in shallow water without fear of getting hung up on hidden sandbars. This came in handy when being pursued by larger warships. Many pirates escaped justice by disappearing into shallow coastal waters and inlets, where bigger, heavier naval vessels could not follow.

Facing page: A model of a two-masted brigantine named the *Lynx*. Brigantines, like sloops, were fast, and could easily sail in shallow coastal waters.

Parts of a Pirate Ship

The *Whydah* was a three-masted, 18-gun ship used by the pirate Sam Bellamy.
Originally used in the slave trade, it was captured by Bellamy as it sailed in the
Bahamas. The *Whydah* was sunk in a huge storm off Cape Cod, Massachusetts,
on April 26, 1717. There were only two survivors out of a crew of 146 men and
boys. Bellamy drowned along with his crew and treasure. In 1984, the wreck was
discovered by underwater archeologists. Artwork by Don Maitz.

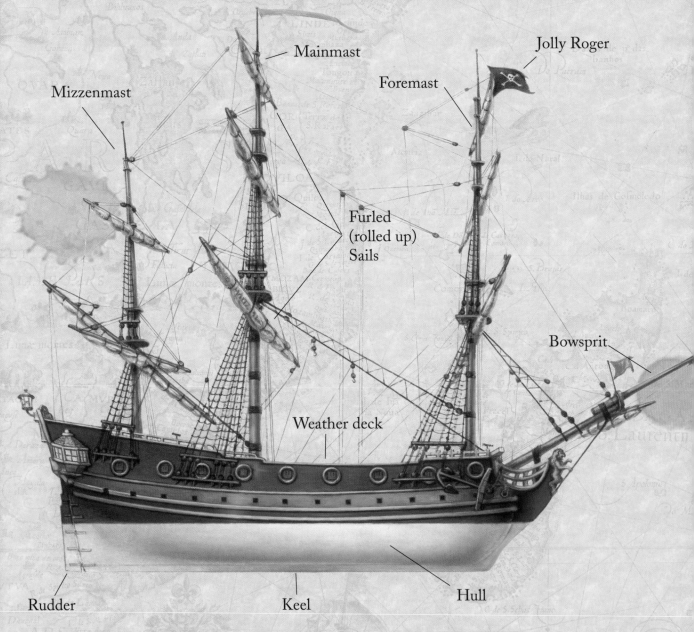

Mainmast

Jolly Roger

Foremast

Mizzenmast

Furled
(rolled up)
Sails

Bowsprit

Weather deck

Rudder

Keel

Hull

Some pirates, such as Blackbeard and Bartholomew Roberts, preferred larger ships, with more cannons. But by and large, most pirates sailed smaller and faster vessels. Sloops were a definite majority of pirate ships, but buccaneers were also quick to steal slightly larger vessels, such as schooners and brigantines, should the opportunity arise.

Pirates kept their ships well maintained. They had to make sure everything was running smoothly, since their very lives depended on fast, seaworthy vessels. Pirate ships were regularly careened in order to clean the hull. To careen a ship, the pirates sailed it to one of hundreds of remote African or Caribbean islands and ran the vessel up onto a shallow sandbar. When the tide went out, the ship leaned over on its keel, the bottom spine of the hull. Workers were then able to scrape off any foreign material, such as barnacles or seaweed. Other crew members attended to the sails, repairing any holes that needed mending. When the tide came back in, the ship was put afloat once more, ready for action. With a smooth hull and full sails, ships were able to cut through the water much faster. Properly maintained pirate sloops were almost always able to catch their prey, especially when their quarry was fat with treasure.

Above: A pirate waits while his ship is careened.

If pirates stole a merchant ship and decided to keep it, they almost certainly had to make some modifications. Space was at a premium aboard most pirate ships. The vessels had to hold many men, additional cannons, and more cargo. To make the necessary changes, some inside partitions, called bulkheads, were pulled down, creating a clear space for the pirates and cannons to move around. The supporting timbers were also strengthened. The upper deck was made "flush." This meant removing raised decks so that the main deck, called the weather deck, was level from bow to stern (front to back), which made a better fighting platform.

Ship Types

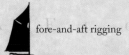 fore-and-aft rigging

 square rigging

Bark

A bark (also spelled barque) was a small, three-masted ship favored by Caribbean pirates because it was fast and could slip close to coastlines, due to its shallow draft. Barks were wide compared to schooners or sloops, which meant they could carry more men and cargo. Most barks held as many as 90 men and 12 cannons

Brig

A brig was a two-masted ship with square rigging on both masts. Brigs were large vessels, carrying up to 100 men, and were popular with pirates who went on long sea voyages, looking for plunder across the Atlantic Ocean. A variation was the brigantine, which had fore-and-aft rigging on the mainmast (see example on page 17).

Schooner

A schooner was a variation of the sloop, common in American and Caribbean waters starting in the 18th century. Schooners had narrow hulls, with fore-and-aft rigging on two masts. Their large spread of sail, compared to their hull size, made them very fast. They carried about 75 men and 8 cannons, but had a short cruising range.

Ship illustrations courtesy *Pirates of the Burning Sea*/Flying Lab Software.

Frigate

A frigate was a man-of-war, with three masts and full square rigging. It was smaller than a ship of the line, but still carried up to 40 cannons. Frigates packed a powerful punch, and they were relatively fast. Their speed and maneuverability made them excellent as pirate hunters.

Galleon

The Spanish galleon was the apple in every pirate's greedy eye. Loaded with gold, silver, and jewels on their way home to Spain from the New World, galleons were slow and vulnerable. They were heavily armed, however, carrying up to 74 cannons and 200 men. Galleons usually traveled in convoys for added protection.

Sloop

The sloop was the most popular pirate vessel of the 17th and 18th centuries. Sloops typically had a single mast, with fore-and-aft rigging. Their large spread of sail, compared to their narrow hulls, made them fast. They also had shallow drafts, which helped them operate close to land. Sloops could carry up to 75 men, and were armed with about 14 cannons.

The Jolly Roger

If there's one thing in the world that people identify pirates with, it is the Jolly Roger. The very thought of a ship with a pirate flag flapping in the wind atop its mast sent fear into the hearts of most merchant-vessel captains and crew. This is precisely what the pirates wanted. Fear was a pirate's greatest weapon.

During the Golden Age of Piracy, buccaneers ruled by intimidation. They backed it up with a huge display of force and a maniacal fighting style (Arrrrr!), but fear played a big part in any pirate's success. The pirate flag, with its various symbols of death and destruction, was designed specifically to make a pirate's foes give up without a fight. This avoided any unnecessary bloodshed, or destruction of cargo, which the pirates naturally wanted preserved in the best possible condition. This early form of psychological warfare worked wonders, especially if the pirate had a reputation for bloodthirstiness. The flags of Blackbeard and Bartholomew Roberts were especially feared.

In June 1720, Bartholomew Roberts and his crew sailed into the harbor of Trepassey, Newfoundland, with his black flag flying. One of Roberts' Jolly Rogers showed a man and a skeleton sharing a drink and toasting death. Roberts had a mean reputation for showing no mercy if his attacks were resisted, and sometimes even when there was no resistance made at all. The people of Trepassey, once they realized it was Roberts sailing into their harbor, panicked and fled the town.

No one is quite sure when pirates began flying flags with the skull and crossbones. A skull, or "death's head," has been a symbol of death since the Middle Ages. Some pirates, however, had flags that showed bleeding hearts, whole skeletons, or hands gripping swords. Not all flags were black; many were blood red. The message of all these variations was the same: death was approaching. Surrender or suffer the consequences.

By about 1700, many pirates had settled on a skull and crossbones, or some similar variation, as their personal flag. Edward England flew a plain skull and bones on a black flag, while Jack Rackham preferred a skull over a pair of crossed swords. Some pirates continued to be creative. Blackbeard's flag showed a skeleton holding a spear, stabbing at a bleeding heart.

The origin of the name "Jolly Roger" is elusive. Some people believe it is an English translation of a French phrase, *jolie rouge*, which means "pretty red," referring to a blood-red flag. Jolly Roger may also be a variation of the name of Ali Raja, a Tamil pirate who sailed in the Indian Ocean. But, as maritime historian David Cordingly writes in his book *Under the Black Flag*, "A third and perhaps more convincing theory is that it was derived from the nickname for the devil, which was 'Old Roger.'"

Right: A collection of pirate flags, and the pirates with whom they are usually associated. These are modern depictions of how the original flags may have looked, based on descriptions in books and eyewitness accounts.

Edward England

Bartholomew Roberts

Blackbeard

Henry Avery

Jack Rackham

Thomas Tew

Cannons

A ship's most fearsome weapons were its cannons. Naval artillery had advanced enough by the beginning of the 17th century that most ships were armed with at least several heavy guns. These were mounted on wheeled carriages that could be moved back and forth for reloading. A small ship such as a sloop might carry 14 cannons, while a massive triple-decker man-of-war often sported more than 100 guns. Cannons were classified by the weight of the shots they fired. The largest cannons, which were mounted on the lowest deck for stability, could hurl a solid lead ball weighing 42 pounds (19 kg) at a target up to 2,000 yards (1,829 m) away. More commonly, ships were armed with 6-pounder (2.7-kg) and 24-pounder (10.9-kg) cannons, with an effective range between 200 to 500 feet (61 to 152 m). A single cannon might weigh as much as two tons (1,814 kg).

When battling ships got close to each other, they sometimes changed ammunition. Chain shot was simply chains, often with small iron balls attached to the ends, that ripped the enemy's sails to shreds. Sometimes two iron balls were attached with a metal bar, which could easily turn wooden masts to splinters.

Grapeshot was a wicked weapon designed to kill sailors on the decks of enemy vessels. Also called canister shot, it was a metal container filled with small iron balls, stones, glass, or nails. The dread pirate Bartholomew Roberts was killed by grapeshot during a battle in 1722.

Left: A man-of-war with three gun decks.
Facing page: Gunner With Ball by artist Don Maitz.

Battle Tactics

It was a rare pirate that attacked a man-of-war or a heavily armed merchant vessel, especially when sailing in something as small as a sloop. Pirates usually attacked only when they knew they had a good chance of winning the battle. This meant finding lightly armed ships that the buccaneers knew they could outshoot or outrun. Some pirates, such as Bartholomew Roberts, attacked more formidable vessels, but most were content to prey on the weak.

When they attacked, the pirates sailed at an angle, toward the bow or stern of their victim's ship, to avoid any broadsides from the enemy's side cannons. They might run up the flag of a friendly nation to trick their quarry into letting them sail closer. Then, when they closed the gap, the pirates ran up the Jolly Roger, striking fear into the merchant ship's crew.

Below: A pirate captain lies mortally wounded on the deck of his ship.

The merchant captain was then faced with a terrible choice: give up and lose his cargo, or fight. If they lost the battle, the consequences could be terrible. Pirates were very cruel to prisoners who had resisted. On the other hand, captives were sometimes slaughtered whether they had surrendered or not.

From the pirates' point of view, it was always better if their prey gave up without a fight. But pirates were a rough-and-ready bunch, prepared to swing across, cutlasses drawn and pistols primed, if their captain gave the order. After all, there was treasure to be had. Yo ho!

Above: Sailors exchange cannon fire with a pirate vessel.

Glossary

Bahamas
A group of islands in the western Atlantic Ocean, southeast of Florida and north of Cuba. Held as a British colony in the 18th and 19th centuries.

Booty
A pirate word meaning treasure, or plunder.

Broadside
When a warship simultaneously fires all its cannons on one side.

Buccaneers
Men who raided and captured ships, especially off the Spanish coasts of the Americas during the 17th and 18th centuries.

Careen
To bring a ship to shore and heave it down to its side in order to clean or repair the hull.

Caribbean
The islands and area of the Caribbean Sea, roughly the area between Florida and South and Central America.

Cutlass
A short, curved sword having a single sharp edge, often used by sailors.

Dagger
A knife-like weapon with a handle and pointed blade.

Golden Age of Piracy

Roughly the years 1660 to 1740, the era when piracy was at its peak, especially along the coast of colonial America and in the Caribbean. Many former privateers, put out of work as peace spread across Europe, turned to piracy. The lack of a strong, central colonial government led to poor protection of ships at sea, at a time when many vessels carried valuables across the Atlantic Ocean.

Grappling Hook

A hook with multiple prongs attached to a rope, designed to be thrown some distance to take hold of a target. They were used in naval warfare to ensnare the rigging or hull of an enemy ship so it could be drawn in and boarded.

Keel

The stiff center, or spine, of a ship that runs from bow to stern (front to back). It was often made of a hardwood, like teak. The rest of the ship's hull is built upon and supported by the keel.

Man-of-War

Above: Patches by Don Maitz.

A large sailing warship armed with many cannons. These ships were used on the front line of a battle.

Sloop

A fast single-masted sailing vessel with fore-and-aft rigging. Outfitted for war, it had a single gun deck, and usually carried up to 14 cannons. Most pirates preferred sloops because the ships were fast, could sail in shallow water, and were very maneuverable.

Index